James Jackson

Piles, and their treatment

James Jackson

Piles, and their treatment

ISBN/EAN: 9783337865665

Printed in Europe, USA, Canada, Australia, Japan

Cover: Foto ©ninafisch / pixelio.de

More available books at **www.hansebooks.com**

PILES,

AND

THEIR TREATMENT.

BY JAMES C. JACKSON, M. D.,

PHYSICIAN-IN-CHIEF AT "OUR HOME ON THE HILLSIDE,"
DANSVILLE, N. Y.

DANSVILLE, N. Y.
AUSTIN, JACKSON & CO., PUBLISHERS.
1868.

PILES, AND THEIR TREATMENT.

BY JAMES C. JACKSON, M. D.

There is no disease which we have ever had to treat, in which we have had better success than in the treatment of Hemorrhoids, or Piles; and yet no persons have ever come to us with any disease which has received at the hands of the medical profession more empirical management than have those who have come to us afflicted with Piles. Very much has been written, and that dogmatically and ignorantly, in regard to Hemorrhoids. The treatment usually administered by physicians is quite out of the line of scientific certainty, and is not only not productive of cure, but, oftener than otherwise, involves complications of a constitutional and very serious nature. I cannot count up the number of cases where metastatic, or substitutive action, has resulted in cases of Piles, from the treatment administered for their cure. I have known severe congestions of the liver to result from the administration of so-called remedial agencies for their cure. I have also known severe hemorrhages of the lungs to result from the sudden cessation of the flux of the bowels, under the remedies employed to cure the Piles. I have also, in several instances, known severe congestions of the brain to take place, in two or three instances inducing complete coma, within eight-and-forty hours after medical appliances for Piles had been made.

I have treated, during the time in which I have been in charge of a Health Infirmary, over seven hundred and fifty cases of Piles. The majority of persons suffering from the disease, (and the worst cases which I have ever had to treat,) have been males. I am disposed to think that during the period of menstruation woman is much less susceptible to Hemorrhoids than man, though, from the time the change of life takes place, there is, perhaps, no essential difference in their liabilities, other things being equal.

The disease has been, by a distinguished writer, defined as follows : "Pain, with great weight, heat, or other uneasy sensation in the rectum and anus, accompanied or followed by tumors in these parts, or by a flow of blood, recurring at intervals, and sometimes periodically."

Persons afflicted with Piles, owing to the injudicious method of treatment employed by the medical faculty, generally lack intelligence to understand the consequences which may result from ill-management, and therefore are left in their ignorance to use all sorts of empirical applications, in the hope that they may be cured by some of them. Of quack medicines, which are found in every drug-store, grocery-store, and grocery-bazaar, there are no specifics offered for the cure of any disease so numerous as panaceas for Piles. There are now advertised, in the various newspapers in this country, over seventy-five specific remedies for the cure of this disease, and it may be said with entire truth, that there is not one of them but what adds to the difficulty under which the person labors ; or, if under their use relief is produced, it is either merely temporary, or, if permanent, is made so by the substitution of some other disease for the Piles, more injurious to health and life, and altogether more difficult to manage under judicious means, than the Piles themselves are. It is estimated there are over four millions of dollars in value of Piles specifics sold annually in the United States, and that of this sum twenty-five per cent.

is net profit, thus making a million of dollars clear gain from the sale of these panaceas. Divide this among the seventy-five different varieties of specific remedies, and you have about twelve thousand dollars annual profit to each one, from the sale of this class of medicines alone.

From my own professional observation, I feel qualified to say, that at least ninety out of each hundred persons who use these specifics for the cure of their piliary difficulties, are decidedly injured by their use, and that the remaining ten, though not sensibly injured, are not sensibly benefited. The reason for this universal failure to cure the Piles by specific application, grows out of an entire misapprehension of the nature of the disease. For this misunderstanding, physicians of learning and skill are somewhat responsible. Under their practice they have led the people to take on the impression, at least, that the disease is local in its origin, as well as in its nature; whereas the actual truth is that Piles are always of a secondary nature, —never original, but always derivable from or dependent upon some one or other morbid conditions of the system. Generally speaking, the disease is the product of originally deranged conditions of the stomach and liver. Under the efforts of the patient or his physicians to relieve himself of these by powerful medicines, drastic in their nature, constipation takes place, and subsequently thereto inflammation of the very lower portion of the bowels, called the rectum, sets in, more or less active at first in its character, but after a while becoming passive, resulting in tumorous growths in the inner coat of the bowel, which give to the disease the name of Hemorrhoids.

Where the disease does not originate in the taking into the stomach of poisonous medicaments, it is very apt to occur where the subject is a thinker, of sedentary habits, educated to the use of concentrated, highly seasoned, and stimulating food, without any regulation of habit of stool, and, not unlikely, neglectful of cleanliness of skin. Of course, to sit

*

still, as in the case supposed, day after day, to eat stimulating food, concentrated in its nature,—thus leaving but very little factitious matter to pass through the alimentary canal, helping to create fecal bulk, while nervous energy is drawn away from the stomach, liver and bowels by intellectual task-work,—is to so derange the relation between the functional exercise of the bowels and the nervous energy upon which such activity depends, as at length to leave the bowels decidedly deficient in vitalization. Congestions of the blood-vessels of the parts under such processes having long existed, at length morbid or tumorous growths ensue, which become excessively painful whenever the persons pass to stool, the veins become large, and under the pressure of the sphincter muscle, in an attempt to move the bowels, become so overloaded with blood that effusion takes place from their coats, and the person has what is called Bleeding-Piles.

Now every organ in the human body becomes strengthened or weakened by habit, as the case may be. When a person has suffered from bleeding of the bowels a number of times, a predisposition to bleed gradually establishes itself, by-and-by this becomes habitual, and, under unfavorable conditions arising from constipation, the habit becomes an active and ever-present one, so that each time the person goes to stool a passage of the bowels is attended with a flow of blood from the rectal veins. This may be more or less debilitating and dangerous. In many instances it is, in the long run, quite destructive of physical vigor. In some instances it endangers life. There have been reported by medical men, through the medical journals in the country, instances not a few of persons bleeding to death while at stool.

The general character and symptoms of Hemorrhoids may be described by slight pain, or heat, connected with weight, or fullness, at the extremity of the lower bowel, or higher up across the sacrum, with, sometimes, sharp, darting pains, extending into the perineal region, and attended with bearing down, or severe pain at stool. Not unfrequently is an added sensibility of the urethra and neck of the bladder established, and, in women, there is such a bearing down pain, low down in front, as to make them mistake the disease for prolapsus of the womb, which is another and quite different disease. A great many cases of supposed falling of the womb have come under my professional care, when, upon a close diagnosis of the case, it was proved certain that the persons supposed thus to be suffering had nothing but blind piles, with some little irritation of the neck of the bladder and the neck of the womb. In the early stages of Piles, the first indication is a slight coloring of the fæces with blood of a bright color. Whenever this takes place, almost always it may be regarded as critical. Thereafter the indications temporarily subside. When, however, this discharge does not take place, while as yet it is evident that the person is suffering from Piles, he may rest assured that tumors larger or lesser in size have begun their formation, and that in time, when at stool, they will appear upon the turning down of the bowel. These tumors, as they grow, are accompanied by a pricking, or an itching sensation, so that one has the feeling of small ascarides, or pin-worms, in the bowel. Many persons suppose themselves to be troubled with worms, when they have them not,—the feeling being the result of the growth of the hemorrhoids in the rectal passage. In the early stages, these tumors sometimes remain dry, or the fæces are covered with a serum. After a while, the symptoms all disappear, and the person supposes himself well; but no sooner does he take this satisfaction to himself than they re-appear, in added growth and with additional suffering. When this takes place, persons thus afflicted suffer more when standing, or walking, or sitting, and the pain oftentimes extends down the inside of the thighs, occasionally darting clear down to the feet, and sometimes along their bottoms to the balls of the feet;

then blood flows in larger quantity than at first, the tumors being larger. When they disappear they leave corrugated flaps of skin, so that there is a serrated condition of the bowel at its termination. The disease originating, as I have said, in derangements of the stomach, liver and skin, oftentimes, especially in persons of highly nervous organizations, results in decided impairment of the general health. You will find such persons to be subjected to bloodlessness of the external skin, inducing chilliness, alternating with flushes of heat, and, sooner or later, attended with great pallor of countenance and an inability to exercise. Labor, which formerly was a pleasure, becomes a burden, and intellectual activity seems to be entirely beyond the control of the person's will. For it, he is dependent upon the introduction into his circulation of stimulating drinks, —they only reacting on the inflamed conditions of the bowels to add to the disability to relieve the patient. Thus the whole thing passes in a regular current, resulting steadily, though sometimes at lengthened intervals, in diminution of normal power, until, after a while, the subject becomes the victim, not only of diseased conditions of the rectum, but of such general derangement that to him life is of little or no comfort, unless under the hope that he may be relieved of his maladies. Not unfrequently, in scrofulous constitutions, Piles are associated with highly sensitive, if not actually morbid conditions of the lungs. Wherever such sympathy exists, the lungs are temporarily relieved from any overburdened conditions which congestion induces, by a bleeding of the bowels; but if the bleeding is sufficiently extended to act upon the general system in a debilitating manner, then, when reaction comes, the person of weak, or diseased lungs, is all the more weakened and debilitated in lungs thereby.

t Dr. Copland, in his Dissertation on Piles, says, "that until lately hemorrhoids were divided into internal and external, or into Bleeding and Blind Piles, according to their situation and

to their connection with the sanguineous discharge. He thinks
that there are three kinds of tumors, differing essentially, both
in their structure and appearance. The first, or most common
kind, is first seen in the form of fleshy tubercles of a brownish,
or pale red color, situated in the anus, or descending from the
rectum. When these tumors are external, they are paler and
more elastic, and are infiltrated by serum."

" The next formation of tumors is caused by a varicose state
of the veins of the rectum. They seldom attract attention
until they have made some progress ; for the distention takes
place slowly. They are not so disposed to enlarge at particular
periods, and are more permanent and less painful than the first
form. Commonly they are of a dark, or bluish color. When
compressed by the finger they become sensibly less, but return
to their former state when the pressure is removed."

" The third form differs from either of the others in being
soft and spongy to the touch, with distinct vessels on the sur-
face of a purplish color. At stool one, or two, or more of
these tumors generally protrude. In the early stages of the
disease the protruded parts retire spontaneously, but in ad-
vanced stages they require to be replaced by the hand. Evac-
uation of the bowel, in this, is followed by pain, which, especially when the disease is prolonged, does not cease for a number
of hours, and is attended by losses of blood which sometimes
occasion ex-sanguine exhaustion."

In my own practice, I have found the hemorrhoidal dischar-
ges to be extremely various, though, in many instances, they
return with periodical exactness. In some instances, with
women, the hemorrhoidal takes the place of the menstrual discharge, particularly when persons have arrived at change of
life ; and then it is almost sure to assume a periodical form. In
different persons the pain of hemorrhoids varies decidedly.
With some it is almost unintermittent ; others have an aggra-
vation of it whenever they have a passage of the bowels. With

some persons it is eased under severe pressure, while with others it is increased. I have known a great many persons to have hemorrhoidal attacks come on, as the result of slight attacks of colic, and in instances not a few have the pains occurred with severe bleeding, when the subjects of them have been particularly excited in mind for a length of time.

Accompanying the existence of hemorrhoids there is often a severe irritation of the neck of the bladder and of the prostate gland in males, while in females there is, as I have already noticed, a decided congestion of the neck of the uterus, ultimately passing into a chronic inflammation, with such bearing down sensations as to make the person feel as if she were suffering from decided falling of the uterus.

The more remote consequences from the existence of hemorrhoids, which have been witnessed in my practice, have been Prolapsus Ani, with such irritation of other organs adjacent to the bowels, as not unfrequently to produce very severe distress.

My treatment in Piles has been, for the most part, constitutional. I regard them, in general, as of a secondary nature, originating, usually, in great derangement of the stomach, liver, bowels and external skin. Wherever, therefore, I have had to do with the disease, in the main the treatment has been such as would naturally be indicated under such diagnosis.

We have to treat two classes of persons who suffer from Piles.

1st. Those who are thinkers, of sedentary habit, and careless eaters.

2d. Persons of active life, who are gluttonous in their dietetic habits, while at the same time they are neglectful of the calls of nature, in reference to relieving the bowels of whatever fecal matter may have come within their walls.

It may not be uninteresting to the readers of this tract to have me report two or three cases, succinctly, by way of illustrating in general our methods of treatment.

CASE I.

In the year 1851, there came to my house a young man who had been suffering intensely, and for a number of years, from Piles. He had been a gross liver, was at the time such a drinker of ardent spirits as almost to pass the line of moderation, in the common meaning of that phrase, and a tobacco chewer and smoker. His case, in some of its aspects, was the most remarkable I have ever had to treat. For nearly four months after he came to our house, he never had a movement of the bowels without passing blood in such quantities as greatly to deplete and exsanguine him. To that degree did the bleeding take place that his skin became more thoroughly bloodless and pallid than that of any other person I have ever seen.

My treatment was injections, to enable him to pass the matter of the bowels without strain, then immediately to turn the bowel back by hand pressure, to set him down in a sitz-bath, at 80 deg., for twenty minutes, and then let him lie in bed for one or two hours. Every day I gave him a thorough ablution of the whole body, attended with vigorous dry hand-rubbing after the water had been wiped off with a sheet. Satisfied that he never could be cured without change in his dietetic and beverage habits, I took away from him all stimulating foods and drinks, and gave him soft water only as a drink. After about four months of treatment the hemorrhoidal tumors became suppurated, broke, and discharged large quantities of matter. At this time he was very thin in flesh, and quite feeble. Many persons thought that he would die; but such was my confidence in Nature and her recuperative efforts, that I did not yield my conviction that he would ultimately get well; and after the suppuration of the hemorrhoids took place the bleeding ceased entirely, the young man's bowels became regular, his appetite was natural, and in six months from the time that he came to us he left our house much improved, and within four months after he left us he was in the enjoyment of as fine health as a man could ask, and within one year was weighing one hundred and seventy pounds.

CASE II.

A Philadelphia gentleman came to us who had had Piles twenty years, and, to use his own language, had suffered pangs worse than death itself. He was in feeble health, carried with him a most thoroughly alabaster look,—a sort of dead, sallowish white, indicative of great bloodlessness of the general system.

He was treated on constitutional grounds. On two days in the week, he took a half-bath, at a temperature of 85 deg., one minute. On one day in the week, he took a pack which enveloped his whole body in a wet sheet, lying in it from thirty to forty minutes, and upon coming out he passed into a bath at a temperature of 82 deg., for one minute, rubbed by two attendants, when taken out wiped dry, and put to bed. Three days in the week he took a sitz-bath at 85 deg., ten minutes; 80 deg., five minutes; followed by wiping, at the hand of an attendant. He wore abdominal bandages night and day, wet all around all the time. His head was covered, during the day, with a wet head-cap. His appetite, which was poor, gradually increased in intensity, and we finally put him upon a fruit and grain diet exclusively. In the course of seven or eight months, he was so well that when he left us he bore testimonies to our success, and his recovery was everywhere regarded by those who knew him as most remarkable.

CASE III.

A gentleman living in one of the western cities, who had been a great sufferer from hemorrhoids for many years, came to us as a patient. Perhaps from the growth of this particular structure he had suffered more than any other patient whom I have ever treated. Connected with his Piles there was such torpidity of liver as to indicate very great derangement of that organ,—the skin being of a decidedly yellow hue, so that he looked like a light-colored yellow Indian. His health had become greatly impaired under his disease, and he came to us and was treated by us for some six or eight months, during which time his skin became white, his blood increased in quantity, and the confidence of his friends in his recovery was greatly enhanced. When he left us, his improvement had been so great as to cheer us with the almost sure prospect of his entire recovery. We have heard since from him, and learn that he is in good health and able to perform a great deal of business.

———

Let these rules, then, be laid down for the treatment of Piles :

Purgatives should never be taken. Persons who take internal medicine for Piles make a mistake. No one is ever benefitted by them. Nor is there any real benefit derivable from any one of the panaceas. Quack medicines are all delusions, thorough cheats, doing no good. If one is relieved thereby he is, as I have before stated, more likely than not to have, as a substitute for the Piles, a disease still worse.

2d. Whoever, having Piles, would get rid of them, must eat unstimulating, simple food. Meats, cakes, dressings of rich gravies for the table must be abandoned, and in their place grains and vegetables, simply cooked, and fruits, substituted. Then, if the person is so situated as not to overtax the nervous system by labor or thought, and can give to himself or herself plenty of time in the open air whereby to re-invigorate the blood and make it pure, there is good chance that the person may recover.

If persons would rear their children hygienically, they never would have Piles. If persons having Piles will live hygienically, for the most part they will get well. Surgical operations, which are performed for hemorrhoidal tumors, are of questionable use, and are not justifiable on the score of philosophy or success; for very many of those who seek relief in this way are sorely disappointed. By a person troubled with Piles, hard water should never be used as a drink, nor should anything be done which tends to constipate the bowels. When paroxysms of suffering occur, the best remedy is sitz-baths, followed by a recumbent posture, and during the paroxysms as little food should be taken as may be.

www.ingramcontent.com/pod-product-compliance
Lightning Source LLC
Chambersburg PA
CBHW031159090426
42738CB00008B/1400